Language of water

A MONTH WITH POETRY, AND MORE

ABHRA PAL

A lot of your emotions are expressed in these poems. I believe it is true. The life of water from a simple mist to a heavy downpour, the harder the noise, the heavier the emotions can be compared to, say... Beethoven's sonatas or symphonies, in their crescendos and diminuendos as the composer go through life with all the destinations and deceptions it brings.

— ~

So beautiful, Wow the world could do with more poems like this. I love how you repeat the line and then don't... and then zoom in to the very personal touch.

— ~

Such a flood of visions encaptured within a single drop. One drop of water on a single leaf, reflecting back at us an entire world of love and anguish. Dare I disturb it, for a closer view? What lies within? I fear the chaos that follows when the Gods mock us and riffle their long, bony fingers through the grass -- shattering a million reflected worlds into a rainbow of destruction.

— ~

For my Family, without whom, the book, or any other poem would ever be written

Contents

Preface

Every creative person follows a unique learning curve. Despite my desire to learn creative writing formally, I never had the opportunity to take a class. My academic path and professional career have been far from poetry, or any form of creativity for that matter. Yet it has been a craft that has come naturally to me.

In 2023, I participated in National Poetry Writing Month (NaPoWriMo), a challenge to write a poem a day for the entire month of April. I had previously completed this challenge at the beginning of the pandemic, but I knew it would be difficult this year as I had been struggling with health issues since January. Despite the odds, I went on, and the poems from NaPoWriMo make up a significant portion of this collection.

Why did I push myself to take on this challenge, even when it was difficult? Simply because poetry is my refuge. When life's failures overwhelm me, I turn to poetry.

The title poem, "Language of Water," was highlighted on Medium and made me the top writer in poetry. I chose this title for the collection because I see language, like water, as fluid and adaptable. These poems reflect a moment in time that will never return. I hope you enjoy reading them.

Thank you.

Abhra
October '23

Prologue

> A lifetime
>   is a fountainhead
>   of possibilities
>
> let us choose to be on the right
>   side of love
>
> Shall we?

PART ONE

A Month With Poetry

I lived a month with words.
built a house with poetry
April is a month when we all bled.

All the poems are written in the month of April, in solidarity with creative souls around the world.

Day 1: First Sunday of April

A REMINDER

The first Sunday of April
    a lovely warm sun behind my back
    bakes my skin golden,
warms my fingers
flicking through an old book
and devours its tarnished pages.

Today I put the clock back an hour,
    allow me an extra hour
    to read,
    to sink into written words,
    my favourite bed;
    and hope an old letter
    would slip out of the pages, to my surprise.

Today I stand on my balcony.
    watch people walk by,

I look out at the horizon
for the weather
up there in the hills in the west,
and speculate
what would my week look like?

Australia had a summer that breathed fire,
    stepping into a winter
    that would cool us down,
    awash with fresh rain;
    Today is the penultimate autumn sun
    Before the shivering hits our nerves.

The first Sunday of April reminds me of poetry
    And my father, who left us last summer;
    I dreamed of him again,
    A dream
    That warmed me like the
    Sombre sun.

Today I put the clock back an hour
    and allow me an extra hour
    to cherish
    the treasure trove of memorabilia,
    the last spring
    I spent with my brother.

The book in my hand is as old as poetry
    The pages have turned yellow

but ripe with age,
Sometimes
a hidden letter comes out of it,
and reads me a magic
that will always be around.

Day 2: Reading Between The Lines

❧

A POETIC REFLECTION

How you read poetry tells a lot about you
How you sip every word
The brimming warmth
Against your lips,
You take every word in,
Like the light
That seeps in
In the dark of your bedroom
When you are about to make love,
Your love for written words is, in reality,
your unspent love for love.

How you watch the autumn tells a lot about you,
How you weigh every leaf
Ripe with pigments,
Falling one at a time
Waving in thin air,
As you transcend barriers
And perceive weightlessness

Of your falling heart,
Your love for nature is, in the true sense, a
reminder of your femininity.

A late bloom, a poignant lake, a storm
A foray into emotions
A lush cradle of life,
Poetry, thy name is woman.

Day 3 - The Magic in My Closed Fist

<hr>

FINDING JOY AND RESILIENCE

Whenever I groaned in pain,
    someone magically squeezed in
    a note of freedom and joy
in my closed fist.

Whenever I cried my heart out
    in silence,
    a handful of relief
    and spirit, wondrously
    appeared in my closed fist.

Whenever I winced from a deep cut
    agonised by an old wound
    or, a recluse scar ripped open
    I found unopened gifts
    appearing in my fist
    out of thin air.

. . .

Today I wear a layer of shame,
    a gemstone of self-pity
    and gloat
    a lifetime of misfortune;
    as the pristine jewel of all
    shines on my crest.

Day 4 - Hate is an antithesis

WORDS OVERCOME HURT

People who upset us - bullied us,
    blamed us,
    humiliated us;
people we hate to see eye to eye,
Do they even breathe?

People who belittled us - provoked us,
    exploited and never apologised,
    people we hate to see eye to eye,
    Do they eat, drink
    and celebrate?

Our bridges were burnt,
    trust was misplaced,
    love was unfounded,
    for reasons or not,
    people wronged people.

. . .

People who threatened us - scared us,
    cajoled to do their bidding,
    people who made us silently cry,
    Do they hug their children
    or old parents?

Hate begets hate, but it is no seed
    that will one day grow into a tree
    soothing souls, bearing fruit, healing air
    Hate is an antithesis,
    extend arms, and
    No hate is too far
    from a hug.

Day 5 - Metamorphosis

RENEWAL AND REFLECTION

In Autumn,
    I turn into a tree and
    absorb the calming
yet radiant sun
on my wings,
numb from flying;
I nourish from the fresh rain
knocking on my morning window -
I extend my feet out, soaked
they imbibe the pristine tears,
and then I breathe, all the soot
we have breathed out the year before
to synthesise
the zenith food for the soul
in Autumn
I shed my worries
like old leaves
and harness energy
in my bark,
in preparation

for a harsh cold;
Come winter,
I will reprise a frigid death.

"   Wait,
        was I a tree all along?

Day 6 – My soul has a pocket

UNSENT LETTERS FOR MY FATHER

At the end of a long day,
       I stop by the state library
         sit down on the lawn in front,
set my feet free
from the pain of leather shoes
and soak in the comfort of grass
gently brushing at my feed;
The crowd around me
is chatty, friendly, and relaxed; as
the scents from pubs and restaurants fuse.

"If you are lonely,
        do not look down at your feet;
        instead,
        look up to the sky.."

Said my Dad in all his letters,
    and I would read him
    on the school playground,

bare feet, in shorts, sweaty
the grass playing, waving.

I watch people around me feed pigeons,
   listen to the fluttering of their wings,
   The bells from the trams,
   a constant hum of the crowd,
   I have so many things to write to him.

My feet on the grass, at the end of the day,
   is the next best thing to freedom,
   strong, hardened, seasoned
   the feet are my favourite,
   they got me this far - to half-life.

   "We are sky-speakers,
      not ground-whisperers",

He said, whatever that meant,
   I am writing him a response today,
   "Can you deliver it?" I ask the sky in vain
   clouds are piling up,
   hues are gearing up for sunset.

I lost his letters - all of them,
   but my soul has a pocket
   with his words and cryptic sayings
   tucked in, warmly, fresh and
   close to my chest.

· · ·

Sky whispers back to me tonight.

"Not every letter needs to be sent;
    for some, being written is destiny."

I wave him goodbye and
I fold the paper nicely in my shirt,
my soul has an endless pocket.

Day 7 – Fail with Me

FEAR, UNKNOWNS AND DARKNESS
WITHIN

I have seen fears rain
    worries snoop in with dusk
    and disappearing sunset
I have seen questions in the mirror,
and watched distress
become tomorrow.

We are conditioned to
    fight or flight,
    I freeze from the unknown
    watch questions
    appear in the mirror,
    what do I say to the night?

Nightmare lives
    in the soft bed of my sleep,
    and depression in my pills,
    a would hurts worse

when the wound
travels inside out.

I have seen walls crumble
felt blood that runs cold
I'm not afraid of the dark
outside the window,
the shadow that looms large in me.

Come, speak fear with me,
swing by my woes
fall with me
share the questions on the mirror,
Trust me
No problem lives a hundred years.

A DREAM WITHIN A DREAM

I wake up feeling warm and cozy
    yet a stranger to my own bed
    and the same four walls
I ask the sombre sun, slowly snooping in,
"Where am I?"

Afloat in a wavy pleasure ocean
    I look around
    muscles dance from newfound joy
    "What happened last night?"
    The sun remains shy
    and the light plays at my feet.

I pull the curtains
    and the morning breeze
    brushes past my unruly hair
    "Wait! Am I not fully awake yet
    is it a dream,

within the dream?"
feeling replenished after a long week,
amused,
I head over to the coffee
a fresh brew
oozing aroma of blended and roasted
Arabic and Colombian beans
fuse into my senses.

"I cannot possibly still be dreaming."
    I take my coffee
    and step into the garden,
    the penultimate winter blooms adorn
    a foray of colours
    "Is this even my garden?
    the flowers are brighter than ever."

When I close my eyes
    your hands lay gently on my heart,
    a feminine touch
    perturb my wake
    "What if you never left?"

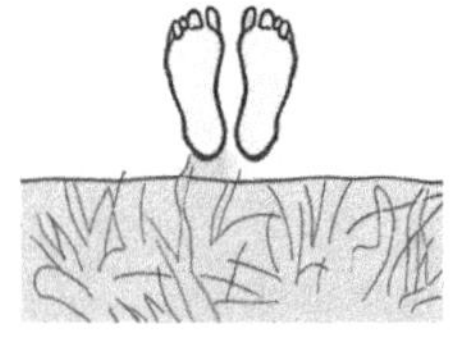

Day 9 - Language of Water

EXPLORING LIFE'S DOORS

You open
a myriad of possibilities
for me
a thousand doors,
some leading to destinations
some towards deceptions
always leaving me curious
to figure out
which one is which.

I calm down
to follow your words
you speak in silence,
a peaceful mist
shaping to a drop
then dancing
on waxy leaves of lotus
each bead
a realm of possibilities.

. . .

I sit down
      next to the window
      to inhale the words you breathe,
      the petrichor exuding from
      a perched earth
      aching
      for the first rain of summer
      there is so much life left
      in this burnt world.

I walk out of the house
      in heavy rain
      to feel your words rise
      from every pore of my skin,
      when the cloudburst
      indulges a lavish pour
      I walk the mud roads,
      like the first
      unknown footfalls of man,
      as a lush green of crops
      wait past the horizon.

You speak in metaphors
      and cryptic life allegories
      that life is water
      in a plethora
      of shapes and forms, and
      I soak in the elixir of tears
      to heal the cuts
      deceptions etched on me.

. . .

You open
      a myriad of possibilities for me,
      when you show me
      wounds heal themselves,
      pain becomes an old friend
      and the most beautiful,
      humane feeling
      is to know
      we are still loved.

Day 10 - Yin and Yang

THE PERFECT CONTRAST

We've seen beginnings that race
until the stale dilutes to pace;
unmet desires plummet from shame
as hardship and necessity prevail.

We've lived relationships to learn,
every bond has a voice to discern;
there must be a good reason why
distance is born, and passion gets wry.

Gifted with an ocean, we couldn't cross
Destiny wouldn't change its course;
the flow of time we couldn't reverse,
stories we've lived without a rehearse.

I am the day, and you are the night.
The perfect contrast just feels right;

I start my day; you bid yours goodbye,
There must be an ideal reason why.

We voice ancient forces' anthem
    Futile apart, potent in tandem;
    wrath of the sun and the moon's grace,
    endurance and nurture do their dance.

We are better off as yin and yang,
    we built our bridge, felt our pang;
    There must be a perfect reason why
    we honed our love and didn't die.

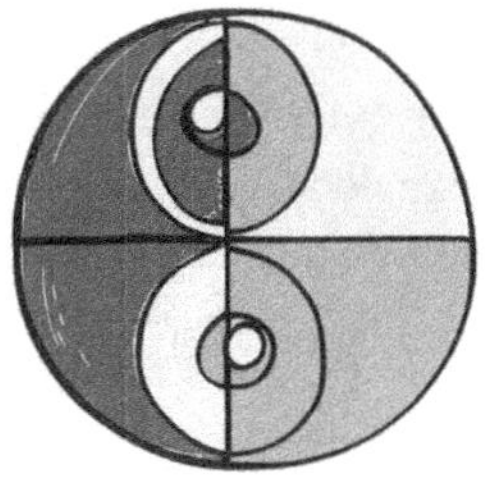

Day 11 - A Tiramisu of Identities

A BRIDGE OF BORROWED IDENTITIES

Today
    I'll borrow something from all of you,
    a word you've spoken,
a strand of stray emotion,
a breath you exhaled,
an iota of your psyche,
and see what I turn into.

I picked a myriad of keepsakes
    a wildling
    a letterbox
    a tiramisu
    a pair of glasses
    a confidante.

Some spring, rain, diet, zest, hatred, ethereal pleasures
    smudged some ink, showed me
    how we are a perfect blend

of things that don't matter,
not one identity defines us,
we live in a great melting pot of survival.

Today
    I'll leave something for all of you,
    A small, everlasting rope-bridge
    For you to elevate
    From who you are,
    To who you want to be.

The bridge will sway,
    from the wind of change;
    so long as we have
    a higher self
    to rise to.

Day 12 - Word-weavers

A RICH TAPESTRY OF EMOTIONS

Winter is an outcry for oomph,
    a yen for warmth,
        Making me brace my layers as
Cold gives me a second skin.

Winter is my zen; as I retire
    to my cocoon of comfort,
    I replenish and feed on my reserve,
    As the sun turns lacklustre.

I construct a magical thread
    coiled around my torso,
    Many crave to untangle it,
    But they just can't.

They treasure what I weave,
    rich and exquisite silk;

they are my life's produce,
One that I muster with my verve.

Silkworm is merely a paradigm,
    what you crave is a treasure;
    the crown jewel of emotions from my chest,
    you are just scratching the surface.

Day 13 - Choking On Truth

THE UNAPOLOGETIC SELF

Do you choke on truth?
    at the sight of my naivety
    on a plate served
to relish
with a sauce of mockery,

Do you drink
    a dry, sarcastic laugh
    domineering
    as I cower
    and pick my pieces up.

Do you see a balance?
    in a scale
    unfavourably askew?
    it's no measure
    of your brazen farce.

. . .

I have a seed
    of fearless truth,
    burdened
    under weights
    heavier than air.

I'll serve you pieces of me
    and watch you choke
    Let us have our dance,
    Naked.

Day 14 - Gaia's Tears

A POEM OF LOVE AND GRATITUDE

Gaia, I have sailed and canvased
　　　　your oceans,
　　　　vast and deep;
questioned

"What do they hold besides the water?"

Expanse
Untamed
Serenity
Calamity
Livelihood
What mysteries await our wonder?

Gaia, the oceans
　　　have been harnessing your releases
　　　since the dawn of time,
　　　the more you suffer and grieve,
　　　the saltier they become.

. . .

Today,
    I will kneel,
    kiss your turf on the lips,
    for a taste of centuries' pain;
    and vow to make you fertile
    with my ashes when I die.

Gaia,
    We have split the world
    into givers and takers,
    forgive us for our greed and waste,
    allow us to rejuvenate you with our remains,
    watch us become your zen

 You have always been our friend.

Day 15 - Rooted in You

NAVIGATING THE SEAS OF LOVE AND PAIN

Sometimes I am quiet,
    poetry quiet,
    Sometimes I am jittery - a boiling pot;
I have many roots,
I am a fruit-bearing tree
I can be cryptic and
my mistrust roams free.

Sometimes I am numb - an emotional mess
    sometimes a benign tree - I harbinger ethos,
    I have many roots,
    and they enmesh so well;
    lost in the grip of the soil
    I battle trapped in my shell.

Sometimes I am a sailor and love a sea woman,
    Sometimes I succumb to my unbearable pain,
    She lures the feelings out,

Let my heart trickle,
our roots grow together, as
She unpicks my riddle.

Sometimes I yield - before the forces of nature,
    Sometimes I crumble, cannot think straight;
    She comes to my rescue,
    To resuscitate our roots;
    As I muster our light, and
    our souls go cahoots.

Day 16 - Crescent Grief

NAVIGATING THROUGH LOSS

You shine at the crossroads
    of my twilight prayer;
      a sky studded with stars, and
feelings we wear.

You chose to part our humdrum existence,
    to live in a magical afterlife,
      you didn't believe in.

Do we paint your passing with light trails?
    Yes, we do, Dad,
      the unspent goodbyes you owe.

I met a waning moon in the dusk,
    too feeble to illuminate a mark;
      an arc of mystery, seen in a while.

. . .

I spotted a crescent in my food
in a famished world, my voice subdued;
I grieved a crescent of your smile.

Day 17 - Inking the Protagonist

FILLING THOSE EMPTINESS

The empty pages beckon me with wide arms
they are old pals with an unmet hug
they lure me into magic realism;
creator and creation become one,
The blank pages are not empty anymore.

Some parts of me have become stories,
emotions gave them a heart,
my triumphs and failures paved the turn of events,
chronicles may have many masks and guises,
Yet the protagonist has always been the time.

My life has been a scorched ocean
I evaporate into purer feelings
to rain, as a verse of solace,
On arid earthlings.

. . .

The empty pages beckon my memories,
    a puddle of rainwater
    a calm shade of comfort
    a scent from childhood; and
    I ink them, anchored in the harbour of losses.

Yes, heartbreak begets words
    sorrow is my love language,
    the blank pages are not empty anymore
    all the scribbles and smudges
    have become eloquently beautiful.

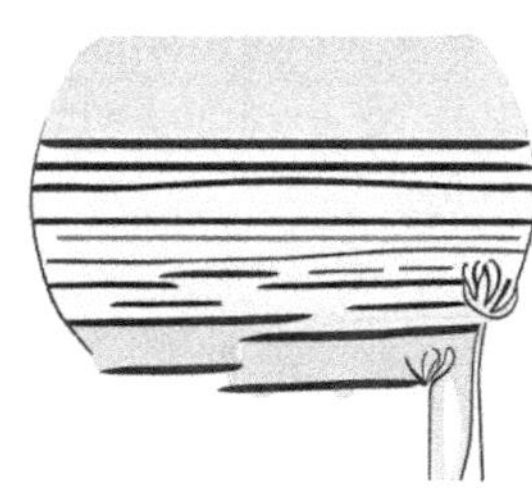

Day 18 – Serendipity

THE UNFATHOMABLE ODDS OF OUR JOURNEY

Do you look back
    on how we were strangers
    before we became lovers?
What are the odds?

Years later, we've come
    to bask in each other's warm sunset.
    At the onset, two more different people
    couldn't be more befitting
    as indiscreetly shattered pieces.

Were we broken to be mended by soul music,
    complete each other's choir?
    We have lived a lifetime of songs
    to watch our plight unfold.

. . .

What if our perception
    of the afterlife was misplaced?
    What if we were placed apart
    To fulfil what we left undone.

Day 19 - Enchantments

A DESTINY OF SCEPTICISM

The world wouldn't
    have us believe in enchantments,
    there is no such thing as sorcery,
and there shouldn't be
a need to romanticise
a gullible's fancy
towards
illusion.

I concur that,
    everybody does,
    we are bread-earners
    in a pragmatic, head-boiled world;
    there is no delusion outside our window
    of hunger and necessities.
    I wouldn't have the world
    believe in enchantments.

. . .

Except,
  the letter I wrote
  twenty years ago,
  and folded the paper onto a paper plane
  to throw out the window,
  reached you years later
  on a rainy morning
  and sprinkled with joy
  washed your face with drizzles
  as you opened the window,
  and you were
  charmed by its earthly spell.

I would know
  if there was any magic left in believing
  and then
  your voice from a choir
  soothes my ear
  ages after you lost your voice.

We are at such a crossroads
  that magic
  is our best bet.

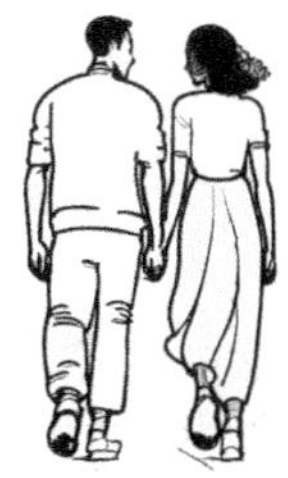

Day 20 - Clandestine

HOME IS WHERE THE HEART IS

Ever felt chilly
    when you were happy?
    or warm
when you were low?
I would imagine not
emotions come in layers
We are only human
to try to hide our feelings
conceal our pain
faces are our worst facades
What gives away
the grim jaws and forbidding eyes?
Do we know our pain?
What is worse than withdrawal?

Ever glimpsed the supermoon
    placidly rising in our backyard?
    snooping behind the unit,
    higher than the Jacaranda tree

beaming the deck
I never get tired of the view.

As age, worry and pain
    descend on my languid wings
    I drink the night as the elixir
    the lucent moon tiptoes
    for a penultimate
    clandestine rendezvous,
    there are such things
    as forever love.

Ever look back to the moment
    when you handed me the key over?
    before we moved in
    to our new house
    the wooden deck
    the garden chairs
    striking purple flowers
    and graceful canopy
    our eloquent tears
    and pearls of our smiles.

When you reminded me
    no matter the pain,
    home is where the heart is,
    our dreams
    may not be dreamed of again,
    the house may fall
    the Jacaranda tree would wither
    yet our clandestine footfalls

into each other's realms
will continue to
unlock hearts
with our key,
everlasting.

A LIFETIME OF VISIONS

Did the dreams have you in awe?
    ethereal visions
        daubed on the back of eyelids
disappeared with the morning
rousing up to warmness,
yet potent enough
to set courses of life.

Did you think our dreams
    would encounter one another?
rendezvous
make acquaintances,
see eye to eye?
no two lovers' dreams are the same
ever.

Dreams are not desires
    they may live in the same house,

want the same backyard, garden,
trees, pets, curtains
eat the same food
hold hands
make love
reproduce
but no two dreams are alike.

I had transcendent visions
of a glass house
a starry sky to look up to
glass walls to discern
a world inside out
a world that can be spelled
a vessel to pour my emotions into
a fresco with myriads of faces.

I was a sucker for written words
a sky painter,
I will forever be
my letters to you
are fragments of my dreams
preserve them, if you can,
gift wrap my journals
with your cherished
wrapping papers.

I will leave
a lifetime of dreams
behind,
an heirloom

to remain locked
for the right key.

I will leave no key behind though
    No two dreams are alike
    when the time comes
    you will understand
    and find me near Southern Cross
    but you will need to build
    your own glass house.

MY COLOUR PALETTE

We see crumbling walls in the news
devasted cities,
lost wars,
refugees queuing up at borders
earth-shattering screams   –
generations plagued by mosquitoes
the world seems to crumble down on us,
we ache, perturb and scream
screams that get trapped
and echo as hateful reminders,
let it thaw, and you'll see
the shoot of peace coming out in silence,
We forget the best thing
we have created — home.

All the small sacrifices we've made
skipping a snow holiday resort,
a train ride along the coastline,

the blue mountains,
a fancy Christmas dinner,
a jacket on the window of a luxury shopping mall,
a new car
No pocket is bottomless,
scarcity, too, is a fire that burns in silence,
compromises are a means to an end, but
we must remember the best thing
we have created — home.

Ever noticed,
    The fire on the stove burns as colourfully,
    as the bushfires that ravage the land?
    the brilliance of flames seized
    the fancy of artists;
    fire is, at best, a nerve-wracking reminder,
    but there is no colour,
    it is our doomed destiny
    to be drawn towards
    the ultimate end;
    the same fire will burn us to ashes,
    and yet, we will still have something
    we have built — a home.

Our home is a box of crayons,
    some blend well with others,
    some don't;
    We have emotions as rich as fall colours,
    At the end of a hard day,
    I stand in front of the mirror
    impotent, flawed and conflicted,

But when I get the crayons out
to give each emotion a colour,
I realise I have all the riches I need,
In this world, my home.

FIND A WAY TO YOUR HEART

Went for a walk at nightfall,
 it was riveting
 to see a purple sky,
with all the hues pouring in,
a crescent moon
rising close to the horizon
above the neighbour's house
along with a luminous Venus,
one could easily mistake it for a star,
like a crown and its jewel
the rare celestial alignment
shimmered.

Tiny footsteps found me a moment of joy
 a way into my heart,
 I'm easily pleased,
 over little things
 no one cares about,
 I'll continue to be,

no matter how dear
happiness can be to come by.

Ever thrown a pebble on a quiet lake?
watch it dance on water,
perturbing the stillness with waves before sinking?
melancholy is an ethereal forever,
life throws pebbles of joy every now and then,
hold them close, while you can.

Serenity is my window
I watch time soar by
altering the world
as fleeting rain smashed on the pane,
I take tiny footsteps every day
as my toes curl from moments of joy.

Day 24 - Faces and Facades

You may have a few facades to choose from
    but I have many faces
    there is an innate difference
how we are both layered.

In the greater scheme of things,
    both are survival instincts
    your reality is one
    masks are armaments;
    my realities are diverse
    my faces manifest
    the essence of the universe
    harnessed in my body.

However cryptic I may sound,
    I admire your gusto,
    the aura of petty deceits,
    you've got an ordinary life

when your guises fall,
it is not the end of the world.

I assimilate many things;
 the sun, air, earth
 I feed on hearts
 I anguish from
 unspent feelings,
 faces are not about me,
 they are music, odes, tales and art,
 humanity needs for continuum.

The hearth of creation,
 the cradle of emotions,
 craftsmanship
 is born off
 the pangs of the prison,
 I am eternally doomed.
 You have to have deceptions to live,
 I have to create a thousand deceptions to live.

A LIFE OF POSSIBILITIES

Life has been a patch of seeds,
    notions, sentiments and potentials,
    planted carefully, subtly or precipitously
by a parent, a friend or the unnamed.

You know more than anyone
    which seeds grew in you,
    which never sprouted
    and precisely those
    who released flammable oils
    to set fire to the habitat
    to open woody seed pods from heat.

Whether they culminate
    or not,
    overabundance
    is in the nature of seeds
    life hasn't stopped for them

but we can, and
offer them a nurture
gift-wrapped.

Peace is a boat
    floating, undulating
    over an endless river of time,
    afloat memories
    love is our much-needed oar
    Come, row with me
    It is the destiny of seeds to grow
    if we let them.

Day 26 - Box of Stories

A POEM FOR POSTERITY

When someone reads this poem years later
the war would have ended
a number would be put to the atrocities
wounded soldiers would have returned home
some would have the means to build lost homes
shells on the streets of Bakhmut will disappear
thick smoke and explosion fog will clear off the air
memorials will be erected
for those who never
made it back home

People hiding in cold tunnels and basements
shaken by unexpected explosions,
would come out unscathed
their suppressed words would need
to see the light of a free world,
even if it is far from perfect;
would we search for voices
under the debris?

.   .   .

Adolescents would question in disbelief,
    "We started a war after a deadly virus?"
    maps would get a break from constant fiddling
    books will need an upgrade
    by a new world order,
    regimes lost
    will survive a mention.

When someone reads this poem years later,
    some will invariably ask
    "Is history accurately written?"
    after all, writers are only human
    prone to fallacies
    coerced by regimes under the threat of livelihood,
    some names would be engraved
    but no plaque has space to unfurl
    the life stories of those
    who never came back.

Those who didn't go to the war,
    will have a box of stories
    adolescents will ask veterans
    "How many battles have you fought within?"
    they will not comprehend war,
    with a lot on their plate
    they will be plagued by
    mistakes of our time.

When someone reads this poem years later

they will raise the flags
commemorate bravery
with drums and fire,
listen to those beats
and the interlude
that would have
silenced many stories
of people who never made it through the war.

Day 27 - Becoming Us

OUR RIVER HOME

What if I told you
as lovers
we are a multi-layered lot,
at the outset,
we're two very different people
percolating through the labyrinth
of sentiments and identities
drowning underneath the sun,
until we find a river
that carries us home.

Have you ever watched your own reflection
on my pupils?

I have
and nothing else can show
my pure ache for you
from our profound want

it is hard to tell
who has the steepest fall,
you breathe quickly
and swallow the silence between us,
covered in lingering twilight
as I watch the night,
become you.

A soothing solitude of silence,
    perturbed by the chiming
    of the grandfather clock,
    the dog's occasional bark
    and the crackling sound of the door
    finds intermittence
    of our libidinal
    stint.

Wet stars upon the moon emerge
    as your ripe lips
    master the craft
    of making me fragile,
    our silhouettes breath
    silence never stopped us
    from sharing.

Together with broken shadows
    we kiss each other
    to sleep,
    two sore doves
    sheltered together

in each other's wings,
and rid our hearts of empty pages, until
a river carries us home.

Day 28 - Dissidents

THE POWER OF TRUTH IN DEATH

The world is not ready for honesty today,
    someday they might;
    if my ashes speak out,
hear them use their silver tongue,
flickering charred remnants of life
that dance and whirl
like ghostly spirits.

Does the
    constant bickering
    stop at death?
    Hate-mongering doesn't;
    the world is not ready for honesty today,
    I better turn around
    in my grave, and
    snooze.

. . .

In the stillness of a casket,
    night doesn't whisper
    confession of sins
    life has given
    darkness a bad name,
    we malign what's beyond us
    for the world is rarely ready for the truth.

A truth we were born with
    equality,
    kindness
    and compassion,
    a truth we aged with
    harmony,
    wisdom
    and a higher self,
    the dark cloud of misogyny
    will continue to shroud
    the gullible
    till they die.

Listen to our ashes speak
    for once,
    ignore the conspicuous nefarious propaganda,
    idolatry can breathe mistrust
    into your being,
    we are a cabal of disillusioned dissidents,
    either we are all sinners
    or none of us
    ever is.

              . . .

If the world is not ready for the truth,
make it.

Day 29 – Rustic Love

EMBRACING THE MUNDANE

We cannot live a fairytale today
  and return to our strifes tomorrow
  the weekday looks good for you
this citrine zest is our rhapsody.

A gentle peck on your cheek,
  a misdemeanour in the kitchen
  a surprising rain and foggy glasses
  the mundane looks good on you.

I will bring you a new orchid
  wrapped in cellophane,
  wishing our walls turn to glasses
  as you twirl from Sunday joy.

I'll make your coffee, and you, my tea,
  play banal songs on the radio

We'll jibber-jabber and waltz
the sweat beads look good on you.

Tapestry is your avocation and
  sounding board is my mirror,
  I'll be amazed by your embroidery
  you can wear my poetry unclad.

We cannot live a fairytale today and
  return to our strifes tomorrow,
  our life is so full of knickknacks
  we wear a rustic love so well.

Day 30 - Paper-born Sentiments

A JOURNEY OF LOVE AND LONGING

We believe in mystical worlds,
    charms that conceal
    immaculate secrets,
strain our hearts and
birth our rivers.

When distance beckons
    I transform into a letter
    don an envelope
    addressed to your lips
    wear a stamp
    slip through
    the slender crevice
    of a letterbox
    journeying to you.

An invite to embrace
    can melt me

pouring down
upon your fervent frame
when senses ache
to conquer distance
our dalliance shape-shift
to bathe in
paper-born
sentiments.

Passion is a self-sustaining star
distance fuels it
while our senses are
honed by the words
that grow,
nurture
and consummate
unmet cravings,
from your lucid touch
gliding through
worn pages;
the paper may decay
but feelings flourish.

Come winter,
	ensconce me
	in your oomph
	close to your chest,
	sing me the unsung adieu
	a reflection of our enunciated bond
	soul to soul,
	mirror to mirror.

PART TWO

The language of us

We are the cause and the reason why,
Love endures, and passion does not die.

The Language of Us

A JOURNEY OF LOVE, HEALING, AND SELF-DISCOVERY

I

We are the cause
    we are the reason why
    love endures
  and passion does not die,
with the strongest oar
we let the boat glide
overcoming waves
and tides with pride.

I waited
  for the tip of your finger
  my needs brew
  as unstated thoughts linger;
  moments prolonged
  as the day closed in,
I met you beyond

an incredible dream.

I found peace
    when I looked into your eyes
    deeper than the ocean
    wider than the skies;
    the water so deep
    I could swim
    but I chose to watch
    the secrets beam.

All of me
    succumbed to all of you,
    your face was aglow
    in the evening hue.
    Your smile,
    a radiant and impending gift,
    adorned a stranger's mask,
    yet truly hedonist.

We showed each other
    a mirror
    in a moment of truth
    both tormented by the past,
    without soothe
    life shattered
    any delusions we had,
    with no expectations,
    how long happiness lasts.

        · · ·

No arm-twisting
    walking on eggshells, no fear
    the first impression
    made the layers disappear,
    our first touch
    gave birth to
    a language of our own,
    made us wear
    the comfort of our bare skin alone.

Hearts sparkled, tears flew
    immersed in the joy,
    there was no need for us
    to hide and remain coy.
    of loves, loss and sunsets that passed,
    we were no strangers
    to a moment of a spark.

Reflection of rain
    was the best makeup you wore,
    a touch on the neck
    made you shudder at the core
    To the key of tears,
    you opened my eyes,
    You were worth the distance in miles.

I took you to a glass house
    in nature's embrace,
    a new beginning
    to shed the past's disgrace.
    a living artwork

poetry on our skin,
Every moment
revealing the layers within.

Ripe with emotions
    we welcomed our stars,
    dreams of bliss descended,
    healing the scars;
    a new world spawned
    at the cradle of your warmth,
    you became a sublime goddess,
    and I transformed.

A lot remains unsaid
    between the lost and dead
    I heard you chirp
    as we lived again,
    We became the cause
    and the reason why
    Love endures
    and passion does not die.

2

We are the cause
　　we are the reason why
　　language is a mystery,
　　and words are shy;
　　Obscure to some
　　even alien to lovers
　　freedom can reveal
　　the bond that matters.

We have hurt ourselves
　　by waiting too long
　　Not knowing for sure
　　where hearts belong
　　a journey through the steps,
　　a string of lovers
　　estranged, fatigued
　　as helplessness hovers.

Across a star-studded sky
　　and blood-red-moon
　　we landed in the evening
　　bound to swoon
　　ill-fated nights
　　that made us lose our voice
　　words finally destined
　　to a bridge of choice.

·　·　·

Our first kiss
    was long, wet, and slow,
    completed us
    with an undying glow;
    we realised destiny
    was no mere tale,
    eternity before us,
    love will always prevail.

As we locked our lips
    hearts found a way
    the world faded
    the earth would sway
    bodies intertwined;
    souls became one,
    A bond that made us
    truly came undone.

The aura of conceits
    clouded us for so long
    pillars of trust were shaken
    not too strong;
    we fought, we screamed
    we turned our back
    finally, we had to
    cut ourselves some slack.

If we could measure
    the letters we bled,
    we would tell you

how many miles we fled
they dripped love,
wore a clandestine cloak
made our world positively baroque.

Evenings grew on us
    our wrinkles became coarse
    our bridge wasn't weakened
    by an invisible force,
    our hair faded into
    salt and pepper
    our kisses still flew
    like a zephyr.

One fine sunset
    amazed by hues
    hand and hand
    we were mesmerised muse,
    you took some pieces
    and sealed them in my hand
    but my firm grip
    couldn't hold the sand.

You whispered in my ears,

    "This is our key,
        this is our forever
        and will always be;

I said,

> We are the cause
>   and the reason why,
>   Love endures,
>   and passion does not die.

3

Forever is a road
    less travelled,
    a beginning
    we often forget;
    two strangers
    destined to cross paths,
    and passions sparked
    from dying embers.

We spoke of an ocean
    I was yet to cross,
    and you had already traversed;
    Yet the seeds
    we planted
    outgrew
    as we gave each other
    the time that was due.

In the spirit of excitement
    we spoke in a language,
    somewhat cryptic
    and hard to follow
    anew to us,
    yet we would wallow.

A language is made up of letters
    sounds, words and styles

the world would have you believe
for us, it was
emotions to perceive.

Sometimes we braced silence
didn't know what to say
sometimes we chose to hold back
needed to cut ourselves
some slack.

We had our qualms
about ourselves
pent-up fatigue
the weight of scorn
inappropriate shame or taboo
yet the roots took deep into.

With much-needed space
our masks fell
so did the need
for false pretence,
we bared our hearts
to the purest need
our language taught
us how to read.

Tears streamed,
and rivers flew
we gave birth to clouds anew
a little piece of the other's heart

became our forever parts.

One morning
    flooded by rain
    I woke up
    to a beautiful dream
    a bridge appeared
    on my window sill
    and magically let
    your sunset
    flow in.

It was hard
    to part ways after that
    we could travel far and beyond,
    No more constrained
    by chains at our feet
    our language showed us
    what to heed.

I wanted to gift you a pendant
    it would transcend
    a forever bond
    an endless dream
    like tears, the joy would beam.

A gift like nothing ever given
    a clandestine prison,
    you cajoled me
    into baring my heart

forever was knocking
at our door
hard.

A rivière of our language reigned
a pendent of illusion
hanging off our forever chain,
we took a road less travelled
the journey left us baffled
strangers across the oceans
formed a bridge of our own stars.

The Arc of Waiting

STORIES OF PATIENCE, MEMORIES,
AND LOVE

An arc of waiting
    with a beginning and an end
     completes our stories
with an intriguing bend,
waiting at the station
for a train you can't yet see,
your feet feel frozen
but your mind goes free.

You hear the sound
    the train may be near
    there's gushing wind
    a force unseen but birr,
    gentle lights shine on the track
    is it the end of a wait
    that was starting to make you slack.

How old were you

when it crossed your mind,
is there a horizon
where do the lines intertwine?
remembering homebound joys unsung
and you still pretend to be young.

Shimmering passing thoughts do rain
watching the beautiful sky
and silhouettes remain,
a gentle breeze caressing you
a lover's touch
that knows no secrets,
no shame ensues.

Far in the city,
the skyline lights;
why is the train late again?
worries from that you can't miss,
a day's fatigue wallows in
the wake of hunger
makes morning makeup
and the facade wears thin.

The warmth of your couch,
the peace of zephyr
your favorite tv show and some banter
sipping a warm soup
and craving for dessert;
sinking in despair
as the vending machines thwart.

. . .

The memory of the first cut
    bleeding, and a cry
    appears out of nowhere
    and you don't know why;
    The first purchase
    from a secret stash
    humble and small,
    or a first high school kiss
    unreciprocated after all.

The first bleed
    the becoming of a woman,
    were much bigger forces at play
    did you reckon?
    the running, the shame
    and a mirror to blame
    full of doubts
    as you are now or even then.

Leaving home for the first time
    newfound freedom in hand
    what does a train have to do
    with memories so grand?
    there's much more
    to reminisce and reflect on,
    a train hums,
    the music of life sings
    a serenade to connect.

From the baby's first kick
    to the labour pain,

interludes with
the massive torrential rain
wary weather alerts
on the news,
interlude with all the gifts
and hearts men brought as cues.

As the final announcement comes,
you are flooded by the first look
at the man you love
all of life's good things
come with a wait
the small price to pay
for all those gifts was great.

An arc of waiting
with a beginning and an end
makes our stories
worth telling to a friend
finds us our freedom,
finds us our home
aboard our happy train
destined we roam.

Ever Present Light

A JOURNEY THROUGH STRUGGLES AND
TRIUMPHS

Love is anywhere but far,
    a light on the way of water;
    a morning in the cold
of uplifting rush,
subtle before the body
warms up to the touch.

The penultimate darkness
    yet you're percipient
    a morning on the horizon
    you're dreaming deep
    in a fleeting state of needs
    that evaporate as you wake.

Submerged in the irony of strife
    as you ruminate
    how vicious is the cycle of life
    half-awake to a realm

mind concocts
eat-sleep-reproduce
but not lost.

A face that you will
    soon have to wear
    adorned with an ornate dress
    and makeup that smear
    a sigh for an impending kiss
    on your neck
    one you nearly always miss.

A child's cry rips
    your moments of musing wry
    a distant bark and your day
    turns into a whimsical waltz;
    in light of fears at bay
    you swoon, and strings strain with your bae.

The cacophonies you drink
    as unwelcome scents sink,
    a train to the city
    clockwork keeps you steady
    a small rip into your soul
    you always thought
    love makes us whole.

Awash with tears
    a lioness in the mirror mews
    shackled by the unruly captivity of truce

a grandmother's tale
a mother's recipe anew
past is the precursor
of hope you pursue.

Omen of the sunset
　　and wings start to tire
　　the day has bore its fruits,
　　obligation to replenish
　　the soul is dire
　　the veins are numb
　　where is the bed of fondness to succumb?

Fatigue plummets and eyelids ink
　　wondering what made life prosperous
　　but eternity shrink
　　Love had a window
　　a joy of the first flight,
　　why would nothing chime,
　　go quietly into the night?

I let you in on my secret
　　I'm not seasonal,
　　an anadromous fish;
　　in search of fertile hearts I drift,
　　tenderness is the water where I breed
　　water me amity
　　and shoots take off my seed.
　　I am love, and I live in you
　　in all your loss
　　a rolling stone

I gather no moss,
in joy or sorrow
or unyielding pain
I never leave you alone
stay unseen but acts of healing remain.

Shut me in the darkest
    closet of your heart
    even pull the curtains
    on the window shut
    try, however, you may
    when the time comes
    my blessings will surface
    and will find a way.

In joy, light or spirit of the day
    come burdens what may,
    a rose in your garden
    will forever bloom
    find a window
    and freedom will loom
    know this and live anew
    I'm anywhere but far from you.

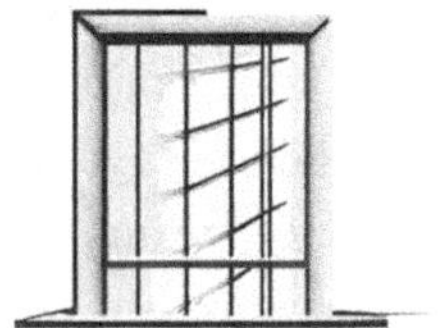

OF TIME AND PLACE AND LIFE

When I walk into the crowd
and look at unfamiliar faces
a gentle hum echoes within.
we walk with a purpose
ignore the myriad of emotions,
the symphony of joy.
distracted, excited, or apathetic,
we brush past clothes and scents
familiar with the unfamiliar.
the masks we don for the day
conceal the unseen tears that flow
little memories tucked inside each drop.

Parted

TWO LOVES OF OUR LIFE

The love we pen and the love we live
parted ways
along a lonely-looking sky

Tantalizing touches
will chime with our potent pledge
to live on as infinite lines

Trepidation rooted in our unsettled flesh
will make us keep questioning,
as we cradle the moon of our peace.

We are water

I.

Leave the window open
    and the lone page
    from a recluse journal
flutters from the strong wind,
gets wet from untimely rain.

Someone you used to know
    someone tethered to your spirit
    relevant anymore or not
    hover in your heart,
    as you let in some wild wind.

Someone perturbed your core
    don't love you back today

or so you feel, yet
floodgates open when
you leave the journal before an open window.

You locked part of your soul away
    wear a mask so well
    someone you used to know,
    wouldn't recognise you at all,
    but you know what?

Masks are no good
    in front of an open window
    and untimely rain.

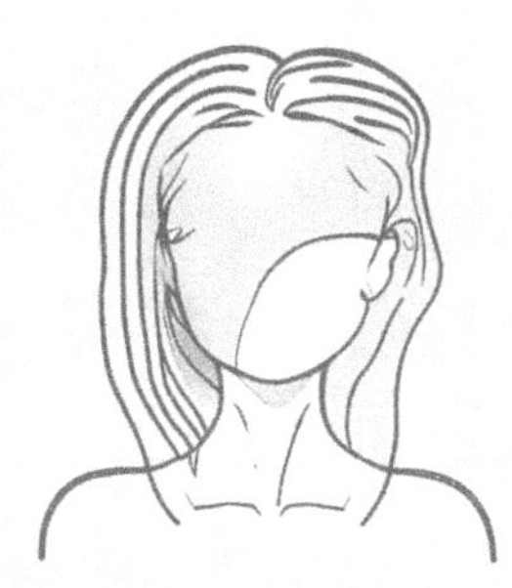

2

As you braid your hair
    in mellow light
    from the parting sun,
    songbirds tell me of letters
    that will remain undone.

When you wake up
    with a splash of gentle dawn
    knocking at our window
    songbirds chirp
    a treasure trove of memorabilia.

You held my hand
    I tasted your tears.
    you pulled my hair
    I tasted your tantrums
    we know how the glaciers form
    how rivers stream
    we have seen
    the ebb and tide
    dance at our feet.

You kept a Dionysian secret
    close to your chest
    we are water, come rain
    we will unfold
    the undying mysteries of love.

The Enchanting Waters

Do you know an ocean?
            of course, you do
            I do and
a gazillion beach lovers
paint joy on a soft bed of sand
and waving summer
freedom
the oceans
they go further than the beaches, though
circumvent our land
at our farthest borders,
harness a plethora of life forms-
we know an ocean or more
all right,
we have one we litter,
defile
we need an ocean
more than we think we need

. . .

Do you know an ocean?
    the current she carries
    the fleeting fauna
    or anchored corals
    the penguin colonies?
    of the drifting ice?
    of course,
    you know an ocean
    the depth
    you dare not surmise
    the salt that has aged
    with her,
    you've seen her outraged,
    outbursts of violent winds;
    wreaking havoc;
    you've feared her worst.
    the oceans
    they go
    deeper and further than
    love and hate, though
    we expend an ocean
    more than
    we think we do.
    as our piety perpetuates
    atlas constricts
    to four walls, and
    the quintessence
    of an ocean's spirit
    comes home.

" O, mother! Thy name is ocean.

Now that you have finished reading this book, there is no harm in sharing a few things about what made it possible.

This year has been a challenging one for me. I faced health issues that agonized me for months, and I was relatively new to the writing platform of Medium, where I was harassed by a few others on a couple of occasions. I was often hospitalized or locked up at home, unable to go anywhere and relying heavily on painkillers. It goes without saying that some of these negative emotions found their way into my poetry.

Despite the many downs, I went through an emotional journey that brought out the purest of me, as always. As I wrote every day on Medium, I received encouraging feedback from readers, which helped me to write.

If you have read my words, you have known me at my weakest and known some of my deepest secrets. The poems will grow old, but the emotions they convey will transcend time.

All I can say is thank you for taking the time to journey with me, it means a lot.

Abhra

About the Author

Abhra Pal was born in a small town near Kolkata, India. He was schooled at the Ramakrishna Mission and went on to attain a degree in Electronics and Communication. He now lives in Melbourne, Australia, where he works full time in IT as a Senior Solution Architect in Financial Services.

As a creative at heart, Abhra has always enjoyed writing and poetry was among his first loves. He has dabbled in it for many years, submitting many items of work to poetry magazines 'Language of water' is his second poetry collection, after 'Words from Isolation'. The poems were initially published in his medium blog, Mon Esprit.

Today, Abhra enjoys his new life in Australia and in his free time enjoys spending lots of it with his young daughter, who has inherited his own creative streak. He also enjoys photography, creative writing in both English and Bengali, watching films and making some of his own as well.

As someone who has travelled widely in his life, including most of India and the UK, Abhra is keen to see other parts of the world that he has not yet found his way to. He is also keen to publish a novel one day, while continuing to pen beautiful poetry that readers can relate to.

You can contact Abhra Pal at: <u>abhra.pal@gmail.com</u>